Dig it:
History from
OBJECTS

# The Greeks

John Malam

PowerKiDS
press.
New York

Published in 2011 by The Rosen Publishing Group Inc.
29 East 21st Street, New York, NY 10010

First Edition

Produced for Wayland by Calcium
Design: Paul Myerscough
Editor: Sarah Eason
Editor for Wayland: Camilla Lloyd
Illustrations: Geoff Ward
Picture Research: Maria Joannou
Consultant: John Malam

Library of Congress Cataloging-in-Publication Data

Malam, John, 1957-
The Greeks / by John Malam. — 1st ed.
    p. cm. — (Dig it: history from objects)
ISBN 978-1-4488-3284-2 (library binding)
1. Greece—Civilization—To 146 B.C. 2. Greece—Antiquities—Juvenile
literature. I. Title.
DF77.M2866 2011
938—dc22

                                        2010023833

Photographs:
Alamy Images: Ivy Close Images 18, The London Art Archive 12; Corbis: Araldo
de Luca 10, The Picture Desk Limited 24b; Dreamstime: Jasmin Krpan 23t, 26c;
Fotolia: Fotografik 7, 26b, Sam Shapiro 3, 20, 27b; Shutterstock: Krechet 21t,
Jozef Sedmak 14, Asier Villafranca 9t, 26t; WizData, inc. 8; The Picture Desk:
Art Archive/Musée du Louvre Paris/Gianni Dagli Orti 16; Topham Picturepoint:
11; Wayland Picture Library: 9b, 17t, 19b, 21b, 22, 23b 24t, 27c; Wikimedia:
6, Matthias Kabel 13t, Marie-Lan Nguyen 4, 5, 13b, 15b, 17b, 19t, 25, 27t,
Bibi Saint-Pol 15t.

Manufactured in China
CPSIA Compliance Information: Batch #WAW1102PK: For Further Information
contact Rosen Publishing, New York, New York at 1-800-237-9932

# Contents

# Who Were the Greeks?

The ancient Greeks lived in a land they called Hellas. Today, we call it Greece. The ancient Greeks created a great **civilization**, in which science, medicine, sports, architecture, and politics were taught and practiced.

## Early Peoples of Greece

Two groups of people lived in ancient Greece about 3,500 years ago. The first was the Minoans, who lived on Crete and other islands near the mainland. They had their own language, which was not Greek. The second group was the Mycenaeans, who lived on the mainland of Greece. They spoke and wrote in an ancient Greek language.

*This gold mask was found in a Mycenean grave. It is called a death mask, and was placed over the face of the dead man.*

## The Mycenaeans

The Mycenaean civilization lasted from 1600 BCE to 1100 BCE. The main town in which the Myceneans lived was called Mycenae. It was surrounded by a wall of huge stones. The wall might have been built to defend Mycenae from attackers. However, it didn't work. By 1100 BCE, the Mycenean towns had been destroyed and the civilization had died out. No one knows for sure why this happened.

**GRAND PALACE**

The Minoan palace at Knossos, Crete, had more than 1,000 rooms.

# The "Golden Age" of Greece

After the Myceneans died out, there was no form of writing in ancient Greece for 300 years. This time is known as the "dark age." Greek civilization then became great from about 500 BCE onward. This was when the Greeks controlled a huge **empire** that stretched from Greece far into Asia.

*Greece has a mainland attached to southeast Europe. It also includes islands in the surrounding seas.*

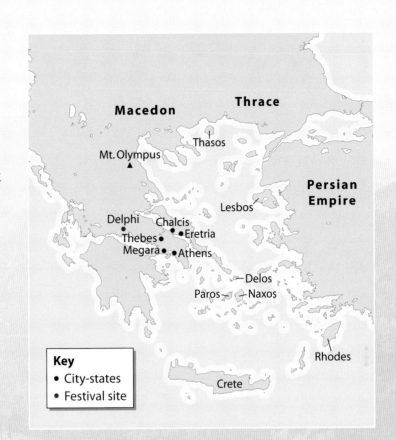

Macedon
Thrace
Thasos
Mt. Olympus
Persian Empire
Lesbos
Delphi
Chalcis
Thebes •Eretria
Megara• •Athens
Delos
Paros Naxos
Rhodes
Crete

**Key**
- City-states
- Festival site

# What Does it Tell Us?

This is a rhyton. It is a container used for pouring or sprinkling liquids at **religious ceremonies**. It was made by the Minoans, who carved a piece of hard stone into the shape of a bull's head. The bull was an important animal in Minoan religion. It was believed to be **sacred**, or holy. There was even a ceremony in which men and women grabbed a bull's horns and then somersaulted over the animal's back.

# City of Athens

Ancient Greece was not like a modern country. Instead of being one country, it was made up of many city-states. These were areas of land controlled by a large city. The most powerful city-state was Athens.

## The City-State of Athens

In the 400s BCE, the city-state of Athens covered a large area of land. Around 75,000 people lived in the city. Another 175,000 people lived in the countryside surrounding the city. Altogether, about 250,000 people lived in the city-state.

## Acropolis and Parthenon

A tall hill overlooked Athens. The Greeks called it an acropolis, which means "'top of the city." Most of Athens' **temples**, **altars**, and sacred statues stood here.

*The Acropolis hill still towers over Athens today, just as it has done for thousands of years. The Parthenon is the largest temple of the Acropolis.*

The largest and most important temple was the Parthenon. It was built between 447 BCE and 432 BCE, in honor of the goddess Athena. A huge statue of Athena stood inside. It was 40 feet (12 meters) high and made of gold, **ivory**, and timber.

**BLOWN UP**

The Parthenon was badly damaged by an explosion in 1687, which blew the roof off.

## The Market

The busiest part of Athens was the market, known as the agora. It was a large square where merchants set up stalls. There they sold everyday goods, from pots and lamps to olive oil, food, and slaves. Around the edges of the square were long buildings called stoa. These were market stalls, shops, and offices. The stoa were open on one side, so shoppers could easily walk in and out.

The Parthenon temple is almost 2,500 years old.

## What Does it Tell Us?

The Parthenon was decorated with a marble frieze. A frieze is a large piece of stone into which pictures have been carved. These are two of the panels from it. The frieze shows a grand **procession** held every year in Athens. It was the city's main festival, when cows were **sacrificed** then burned on the altar in front of the Parthenon. The cooked meat was shared among the people.

# Greek Townhouses

Most ancient Greek houses were built around a central courtyard. They were called courtyard houses. The walls were made of **mud bricks** or stone and rubble. The roof had clay tiles.

## The Courtyard House

From the street, a courtyard house looked like a wall with a doorway. No one could see into the house, which made it private. Small windows also kept the house cool and dark. Most courtyard houses only had a ground floor. All the rooms faced onto the courtyard, which was used like an outside room. This was where children played, meals were cooked, and where visitors were entertained.

## What Does it Tell Us?

Greek houses did not have running water. Instead, water was collected and stored in large pottery jars called hydrias, such as this one, left. Some people were lucky enough to have their own wells in the courtyard of their house, but most people were not. For them, collecting water meant daily visits to the town's fountains or natural springs.

## Inside the House

Rooms inside the house included bedrooms and workrooms, but there were no bathrooms. Instead, people washed with bowls of water. They went to the bathroom in potties, which they emptied into the streets outside their houses. There was very little furniture in the houses and they had no flooring except for bare earth.

## Houses of the Rich

In some ancient Greek towns, courtyard houses have been found that might have belonged to rich people. The floors were made of hard-wearing, small pieces of stone that were set out in patterns. This is called mosaic. These houses also had bathrooms with bathtubs made of baked clay and toilets connected by clay pipes to drains. The drains took waste away from the house.

A model of a very grand house from the city of Olynthus, northeast Greece.

# Farming and Food

Many people in ancient Greece were farmers. It was vital that enough food was grown to feed everyone, so farming was a very important job.

## Little Farms

Ancient Greek farms were small. They had just enough land for one family and their workers. Some of the land was used for growing crops. Farm animals were kept on the rest of the farm.

## Crops and Animals

The main crop was barley. Its grain was used to make bread. Wheat was also grown, but it was less important than barley. Farmers grew many vegetables and fruits. Many farms had an olive forest called an olive grove. Flax was grown for weaving into **linen** to make clothes. Farm animals were sheep, goats, cattle, and pigs. They provided milk, meat, wool, and hides. Bees were kept for honey.

## What Does it Tell Us?

This vase is painted with a picture of people picking olives. They are hitting the branches of the olive tree with long sticks to make the olives fall to the ground. One man has climbed into the tree to pick olives. Nets on the ground catch the falling olives. Olives were crushed into an oil, which was used as a cooking oil or lamp fuel. It was also rubbed on the body.

# Greek Cooking

Ordinary people ate bread, cakes, and porridge. They also ate fruit, vegetables, cheese, and a little meat. At a feast, rich Greeks ate fish, eels, or quail (small birds) with vegetables served in **savory** or sweet sauces. Most people ate only a little meat. This was followed by fruit and nuts and cheese and honey cakes. Wine mixed with water was drunk because the ancient Greeks thought it was unhealthy to drink wine on its own.

*The image on this pot shows an ancient Greek vineyard, with two boys eating grapes. The Greeks grew grapes for food and to make wine.*

## PICKING OLIVES

The olive harvest began in November and ended in March.

*After an evening meal, rich men lay on couches while musicians played to them.*

# Clothes and Crafts

Most ancient Greek towns had an area where craftspeople worked. They were busy places. Here, potters made clay vases, plates, and bowls. These were decorated with paintings of Greek life. Sculptors carved **marble** or **limestone** statues, then painted them in bright colors. Life-sized statues were made from **bronze**, which was also used for jugs, mirrors, swords, and **armor**.

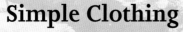 Both of these women are wearing peplos tunics. These were long garments that hung loosely from the shoulders.

## Simple Clothing

Clothes were simple and loose-fitting. Men and women wore a tunic. This was a long piece of clothing that was wrapped around the body. Women wore long tunics and men wore short tunics. On cool days, men and women also wore a cloak over their tunics.

## EVIL SPIRIT

If a pot was broken while it was being made, the potter blamed the demon Syntrips ("Smasher").

## Rich and Poor

Most people wore clothes made from wool or linen. Only the rich could afford clothes made from silk. The clothes of the poor were a cream color, which is the natural color of wool and linen. The rich wore clothes colored with dyes, such as yellow dye, which was made from **saffron**, and purple dye, which was made from a shellfish.

## Makeup and Jewelry

Women wore makeup and gold jewelry. They had long hair, which they tied up with ribbons. Men had short hair and beards.

*Ancient Greek pots are called either "black figure" or "red figure" because the people on them were painted either black or a red-brown color.*

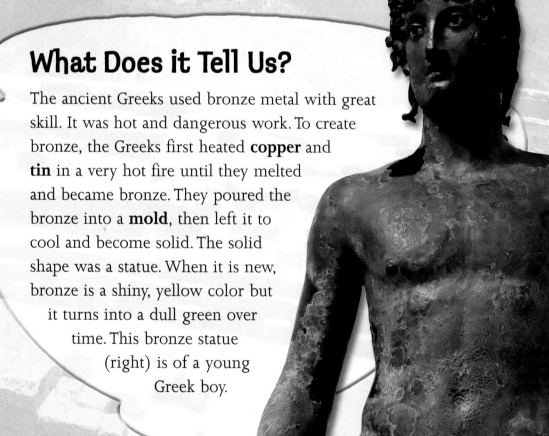

## What Does it Tell Us?

The ancient Greeks used bronze metal with great skill. It was hot and dangerous work. To create bronze, the Greeks first heated **copper** and **tin** in a very hot fire until they melted and became bronze. They poured the bronze into a **mold**, then left it to cool and become solid. The solid shape was a statue. When it is new, bronze is a shiny, yellow color but it turns into a dull green over time. This bronze statue (right) is of a young Greek boy.

# Writing and Myths

The first people in ancient Greece who could write were the Mycenaeans. But when their civilization ended, writing disappeared with them. For the next 300 years, Greece was in a "dark age"—a time without writing.

**STORIES**
Storytellers told stories and poems from memory in loud, singsong voices.

## The Greek Alphabet

The Greeks started writing again between 800 BCE and 750 BCE. They created an alphabet of 24 letters. Letters were written in ink from left to right. The Greeks did not use spaces between words or **punctuation**, and everything was in capital letters.

## Writing Materials

The ancient Greeks carved words into stone, and wrote on a type of paper called **papyrus**. Words were also written on small, wooden boards or tablets. These were coated with a wax. Words were scratched into the wax with a sharp metal stick, called a stylus. After it had been read, the wax was smoothed over so the tablet could be used again.

This clay model shows a man using a stylus to scratch letters into a thin layer of wax on a wooden tablet.

# Greek Myths

The ancient Greeks were great storytellers. They had many stories about gods, heroes, wars, and monsters. These are called myths. To begin with, Greek myths were not written down. They were only spoken by poets and storytellers who could remember them. Then, in the middle of the 700s BCE, the stories were written down for the first time.

 *The painting on this pot shows the myth of Daedalus and Icarus. They tied wings of feathers to their arms, and flew away from Crete.*

## What Does it Tell Us?

This vase is painted with a scene from the story about the hero Odysseus. It shows the moment Odysseus tricked the flying Sirens, whose beautiful singing lured ships onto deadly rocks. The painter must have known the story well, and people who saw the vase would have known which part of the story was shown.

# Children and Schools

In ancient Greece, boys and girls were treated differently. Boys were taught how to behave as good members of their town or city. This was called being a good **citizen**. Girls were prepared for family life.

## Boys vs. Girls

Greek parents wanted to have boys rather than girls. The reason for this was that boys cost their parents less than girls. When girls were married, their parents had to give a gift of money, **goods**, or property to their husband. This was called a dowry. Parents did not need to save up a dowry for their sons.

The picture on this vase shows an ancient Greek classroom. A music lesson is shown on the left and a writing lesson in the center.

## Boys at School

Boys started school when they were seven years old. Parents had to pay the teachers. Rich families could afford to send boys to school until they were 18 years old. Boys from poor families only went for three or four years.

## POPULAR PETS

Children kept pets—dogs and tame hares were their favorites.

## What Does it Tell Us?

Children's toys show that boys and girls in ancient Greece had time to play. This toy is a doll, made from baked clay. It had moving arms and legs. A dress is carved onto the doll, but it may also have had clothes made of cloth. Children also played with spinning tops and hoops, rattles, rocking horses, swings, and seesaws.

*This vase painting shows a toddler sitting on a potty!*

## Girls at Home

Girls did not go to school. Instead, they stayed at home where their mothers taught them how to cook, **weave** wool, and make clothes. It prepared them for married life.

## Becoming Adults

Girls became adults when they were about 14 years old. This was also the age at which they got married. Their parents chose their husbands. Boys became adults when they were about 18, which was when they left school to join the army.

# Gods and Temples

The ancient Greeks believed in many gods. They thought that each god had the power to control a different part of life. People prayed to the gods and left gifts for them at their temples. In return for pleasing the gods this way, Greeks hoped the gods would look after them.

## The Gods of Mount Olympus

The most important gods lived at the top of Mount Olympus, the highest mountain in Greece. The list below shows the main gods.

| | |
|---|---|
| **Aphrodite** | Goddess of love |
| **Apollo** | God of the sun, truth, and healing |
| **Ares** | God of war |
| **Artemis** | Goddess of the moon and childbirth |
| **Athena** | Goddess of war, wisdom, and art |
| **Demeter** | Goddess of grain and fertility |
| **Dionysus** | God of wine and vegetation |
| **Hephaestus** | God of fire and volcanoes |
| **Hera** | Queen of the gods, goddess of women |
| **Hermes** | God of words and travelers |
| **Poseidon** | God of the sea |
| **Zeus** | King of the gods, god of the heavens and weather |

*The weather god Zeus was the most important and powerful of the gods. A thunderbolt was his symbol.*

**HIGHEST PEAK**
Mount Olympus is 9,573 feet (2,918 m) high.

## Greek Temples

Temples were the gods' houses on Earth. Inside each temple was a statue of a god. The Greeks believed the god's spirit lived inside it. When the doors were opened, the statue "looked" out to a courtyard, where **worshipers** gathered with gifts. A gift could be a prayer, or something "real," such as clothing or an animal sacrifice. People hoped that their gifts would please the gods so they would answer their prayers.

The temple of Apollo, at Delphi, was the most important temple in Greece. People from all over the country traveled here.

## What Does it Tell Us?

People sometimes left objects at the temple of the gods, such as this baked-clay sculpture of an ear. The person who left the sculpture may have suffered from an earache and hoped that by leaving the ear sculpture in the temple, the gods might cure him. It shows the person believed the gods could help him.

# The Greeks at War

The ancient Greeks fought many wars. City-states fought each other, but they joined forces to fight a foreign enemy. Many wars were against Persia, in Asia.

This frieze shows soldiers from the army of Alexander the Great attacking Xanthos, a city in Turkey.

## Soldiers and Battles

Greek armies were made up of foot soldiers called hoplites and soldiers who fought on horseback. A hoplite carried a large, round shield, a spear, and an iron sword. The spear was not thrown, but was instead used to jab at the enemy. The sword was used if the spear was lost or broken.

Soldiers wore armor and a helmet for protection. They wore a breastplate to protect their chest and shin pads to protect the front of their legs.

## What Does it Tell Us?

This is a bronze helmet worn by a Greek hoplite. It is made from a single sheet of metal, which was beaten into shape. It was padded on the inside to make it more comfortable to wear. The helmet protected the soldier's whole head, and the back flared out to protect his neck. Tall feathers ran along the top.

## Alexander the Great

Alexander was the leading general in ancient Greece. He was nicknamed "Megas," meaning "the Great." He fought the Persians, who were the enemies of Greece. Between 334 BCE and 323 BCE, Alexander's army defeated the armies of Persia, and anyone else who stood in their way. His greatest battle against the Persians was the Battle of Issus, Turkey, in 333 BCE. The Greeks were heavily outnumbered, but they still beat the Persians.

Alexander created a huge empire that stretched from Greece all the way to India.

This is the body armor of King Philip II, father of Alexander the Great. It was made from iron.

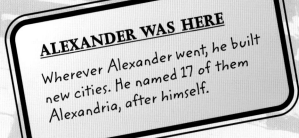

### ALEXANDER WAS HERE

Wherever Alexander went, he built new cities. He named 17 of them Alexandria, after himself.

23

# Entertainment

People stopped work on festival days. They joined in with the celebrations of the gods, they took part in processions or shared meals. Some festivals, such as ones about sports, took place all over Greece and lasted for days.

## Festival of Sports

The most important sport festival was held every four years at Olympia. This was the Olympic Games. Men from all of Greece took part. It was an honor to compete in the games. After the games, a smaller sporting festival was held at Olympia for women. It was called the Heraean Games, after the goddess Hera. There was just one event, a running race.

This bronze *discus* was used by an athlete named Exoidas. It was thrown during sporting competitions.

This statue of a man is made from bronze. His hands are bound with leather strips, which shows he is a boxer.

**WINNER'S WREATH**
A winner at the Olympic Games was crowned with a wreath of laurel leaves.

## Olympic Games Timetable

**Day 1**
- Opening ceremony
- Public and private sacrifices
- Boys' running, wrestling, and boxing contests

**Day 2**
- Chariot races
- Horse races
- Pentathlon (running, discus, jumping, javelin, wrestling)
- Parade of winners
- Singing of hymns

**Day 3**
- Main sacrifices
- Foot races
- Public banquet

**Day 4**
- Wrestling
- Boxing
- Pankration (boxing, kicking, and wrestling combined)
- Race in armor

**Day 5**
- Winners receive their wreaths
- Closing ceremony
- Feasting

## The Theater

Many towns had an outdoor theater. It was a **semicircular** building with hard stone seats, so people brought cushions to sit on. Plays were held in the daytime, on a round area called the orchestra. Actors spoke or sang their parts and music was played. They wore padded costumes and high shoes, so that people in the back seats could see them.

## What Does it Tell Us?

Music was an important part of everyday life in ancient Greece. This vase painting shows a musician playing a stringed instrument called the lyre, which was a little like a harp. Music was played at the theater, as part of religious festivals, and at weddings and funerals. It was also played as storytellers recited poems and tales.

# Quiz

1. **What would you put into a hydria?**
   a. Water
   b. Wine
   c. Olive oil

2. **What was papyrus?**
   a. A piece of clothing
   b. A toy
   c. A type of paper

3. **Who was the king of the gods?**
   a. Poseidon
   b. Zeus
   c. Apollo

4. **What is bronze made from?**
   a. Copper and iron
   b. Copper and tin
   c. Copper and silver

5. **What was a hoplite?**
   a. A foot soldier
   b. A horseman
   c. An athlete

6. **What was the main grain crop?**
   a. Wheat
   b. Barley
   c. Oats

**7. Which island did the Minoans live on?**
 a. Corfu
 b. Crete
 c. Chios

**8. What is the name of the hill overlooking Athens?**
 a. Parthenon
 b. Agora
 c. Acropolis

**9. Where were the Olympic Games held?**
 a. Sparta
 b. Athens
 c. Olympia

**10. How old were boys when they started school?**
 a. Five
 b. Six
 c. Seven

# Timeline

| | |
|---|---|
| **c. 3500** BCE | The Minoan civilization begins on Crete and surrounding islands. |
| **c. 1600** BCE | The Mycenaean civilization begins on mainland Greece; they were the first Greeks. |
| **c. 1650** BCE | Non-Greek writing is used by the Minoans. |
| **c. 1400** BCE | The first Greek writing is used by the Mycenaeans. |
| **c. 1100** BCE | The Minoan and Mycenaean civilizations end. |
| **c. 1050–950** BCE | Some Greeks leave the mainland and settle on islands in the Aegean Sea. |
| **c. 750** BCE | The first Greek alphabet is devised. |
| **c. 750–650** BCE | People move away from Greece and settle around the Mediterranean coast and in Asia Minor (Turkey), where they build Greek colonies. |
| **776** BCE | Traditional date of the first Olympic Games, held at Olympia. |
| **c. 610** BCE | Black-figure pottery first made. |
| **c. 600** BCE | First Greek coins are used. |
| **c. 546** BCE | The Persians conquer Greek colonies in Ionia (in Turkey). |
| **c. 535** BCE | Red-figure pottery first made. |
| **c. 505** BCE | Democracy is introduced in Athens. |
| **490–480** BCE | Wars against the Persians, which the Greeks eventually win. |
| **447–438** BCE | The Parthenon temple is built in Athens. |
| **431–404** BCE | Athens loses a war with Sparta, another city in Greece. |
| **359–336** BCE | Reign of King Philip II of Macedon. |
| **338** BCE | King Philip II becomes the ruler of Greece. |
| **336** BCE | King Philip II dies. His son, Alexander, takes over from him. |
| **334–323** BCE | Alexander the Great conquers Persia and lands farther east, creating an empire for Greece. |
| **323** BCE | Alexander dies, and his empire breaks up. |
| **279** BCE | Greece is invaded by Gauls. |
| **146** BCE | Mainland Greece becomes a province of the Roman Empire. |
| **129** BCE | Greek cities overseas pass to the Romans. |
| **30** BCE | Egypt, the last kingdom of the Greeks, becomes part of the Roman Empire. |

# Glossary

**altar** The part of a holy building where gifts are left for a god or goddess.

**armor** The protective coverings, usually metal, worn by soldiers in battle.

**bronze** A yellowish metal mixed from copper and tin.

**citizen** A Greek who was born a free man, and who had a say in how he wanted his town to be run.

**civilization** A group of people who belong to one country or area.

**copper** A red-colored metal.

**discus** A stone or metal disc thrown by athletes.

**empire** An area of land that includes many countries, ruled by one leader.

**goods** The things that can be bought or sold, such as pots, jewelry, and food.

**ivory** A material from the tusks of an elephant.

**limestone** A cream-colored rock.

**linen** A type of material.

**marble** A hard-wearing white stone used for buildings and statues.

**mold** A hollow shape or container used to shape a liquid into a solid.

**mud bricks** Bricks made from mud mixed with water.

**papyrus** A type of paper made from river reeds.

**procession** When people gather and walk together through the streets.

**punctuation** To break up phrases and sentences of words.

**religious ceremonies** The acts performed for a god or goddess.

**sacred** Something that is holy.

**sacrifice** When an animal is killed for a god or goddess.

**saffron** The part of a variety of crocus, used for dyeing cloth.

**savory** When something tastes salty rather than sweet.

**semicircular** Half a circle.

**temples** The buildings where a god or goddess is worshiped.

**tin** A gray-colored metal.

**weave** To thread lengths of wool into a piece of material.

**worshipers** People who gather to pray to a god.

# Further Information

## Books

**How People Lived in Ancient Greece**
by Colin Hynson
(PowerKids Press, 2008)

**How The Ancient Greeks Lived**
by John Malam
(Gareth Stevens Publishing, 2010)

**The Ancient Greeks**
by Allison Lassieur
(Children's Press, 2005)

## Web Sites

Due to the changing nature of Internet links, PowerKids Press has developed an online list of Web sites related to the subject of this book. This site is updated regularly. Please use this link to access this list: http://www.powerkidslinks.com/dig/greeks

# Index